THE SURGEON'S BRAIN

The Surgeon's Brain

Oscar Upperton

TE HERENGA WAKA
UNIVERSITY PRESS

Te Herenga Waka University Press
Victoria University of Wellington
PO Box 600, Wellington
New Zealand
teherengawakapress.co.nz

Te Herenga Waka University Press
was formerly Victoria University Press.

A catalogue record is available at the National Library of New Zealand.

ISBN 9781776920013

This book was written and published with the support
of Creative New Zealand and the Louis Johnson New Writer's Bursary.

Printed in Singapore by Markono Print Media Pte Ltd

When I was a boy I was told that when I began a story, to begin at the beginning and continue to the end.

—*James Barry*

Contents

Dura Mater | Tough Mother

Arachnoid Mater | Spider Mother

Pia Mater | Tender Mother

DURA MATER

tough mother

Coming into the world

We are never closer. We will not be close again.
This is old to you. You have birthed my brother
and seen babies born many times. For me it is all new.
Space around my arms and legs is new. Cold is new
and painful. Breathing in this way is new, and the world
is so bright, although I have none of these words yet to describe it.

I remember none of what happened.
This is the transcription of an imagined memory.
Why do I do this? Well. I am played out, on my way out. I feel it,
lying in this bed it is like I am dead already.
The sun does not even reach the pane of my window
and no one calls. My lungs are weary with too much breathing
and I have too much space between my chest and the ceiling above,
between my hand and my cup. I know too much.
I have seen in my long career
babies' hands clenched around umbilical cords,
dead babies, dead cords,
live babies, live cords,
dead men, dead women,
live men, live women.

In the room where I am being born you start to bleed
and your aunt, not knowing what else to do,
drags in another sack of sawdust.
You are on the edge of delirium when I come into the world
and your aunt says
you have a girl now, Mary Anne.

You don't have me now, Mary Anne.
I think of the line I have traced around the globe
that led me from that room to this, not so far a distance

but I took the long way around,
the long way around. And now I will tell you of it.

Of an evening

I'm not the kind of friend you'd want to befriend.
Do you know what I do, of an evening? Well.
When the ships come into port there are bodies
on the ships. They must take the bodies
off the ships and if I hide my hair they will
show me a body and tell me how it came to die like that.
Then they ask, where are your parents? and I run, run.
The bodies are much bigger than me, long and puffy,
pickled like fish, and many of them are far from home
but some are coming home to Cork in a bottle.
There are always stories of the dead sailor shut up
in a barrel of rum and the other sailors drink the rum,
and the dead sailor tipped over the side and in the morning
swabbing the deck and his friends too afraid to call to him,
and the plague ships of course they come and anchor
and we wait them out onshore. They are a story telling itself
to itself, a very boring story where the same thing happens
over and over again.
I hide my hair and I say, what's this?
and people tell me things.

Into the forest

Some things I keep secret even from myself.
This town was built on other towns.
Sometimes it's easier to just keep building.
Under that church another church, and they say
people have fished these shores for generations uncounted.

Some things I keep secret even from myself.
The town cats light up the night with yellow eyes
and I'm not supposed to be out of an evening
but I am out of an evening and my feet are wet
and at home Mamma waits beside the fire.

Some things I keep secret even from myself.
I've never seen a forest but sometimes I walk in one
in my dreams, great black trees with twisted branches
and underfoot wet earth and spiders' nests.
This is a forest that covers the world,

and in it live three things: the red foxes that dislike rain,
the innumerable silver spiders, and me, numerable
I think, but when I turn to regard the path behind me
I am there. Each step of me is frozen in place,
curls of earth sticking to the soles of my feet.

Some things I keep secret even from myself.
I didn't want done to me the things that were done to me.
But the sun rises and you say, well.
Only you don't say it. You never say it.

Rent

Rent is the constant word and I hear it like a song.
I go tripping around the house, tidying, cleaning, cleaning,
and I think rent, rent, rent.

Father's hair is falling out in patches and his shirt is all over patches
and I think he is ill. Because we are Catholic he has lost his position.
There has been a decree.

Mamma says it's an ill wind but she won't finish her sentence
and so I think about this ill wind circling the house,
testing our defences.
It's an ill wind all right.
My brother snores for hours and I hear him through the wall,
ill wind in and ill wind out,
and then he coughs and settles.

Mamma says I'll have to maid for someone which means going away
to clean another family's house and sleep in a cupboard.
I say I don't think that would suit me. I say I would rather take a ship
across the sea than a farmer's cart or a broken-winded horse
up a dirt track and into the *countryside*. I say perhaps I'll be a soldier
and she covers her eyes with her hands and breathes
like soon there will be a decree and she won't be allowed any longer.

Father says this all will pass, he just has to balance things out;
one more loan would do it, to cover the rest,
but a lot of men are coming to the house
and when they come Mamma pushes me under the table
and follows me herself
and then one day Father is gone.
Mamma says he must have paid passage to England but in my head
he is running, running, running;

it is morning and mist floats on the river
as he runs out, out, out, into the countryside.

Marriage

People keep using that word around me. I don't know how it relates
except it's always about money, and I need money
so maybe I should listen.
Marriage seems to be a horse and cart venture.
I am frightened of horses wearing blinkers
(flat leather eyes)
and horses with their heads covered, horses that are *difficult to handle*,
horses that *misbehave*; their heads are put in sacks
and they go still all over.
These sacks are called blinders for an obvious reason.
It has always been a fear of mine to lose my sight,
ever since my uncle told me I had eyes so sharp they would cut,
and I thought he meant *be cut*, that my eyes were so sharp
as to inspire surgery and theft. In a bag my eyes would be safe
but useless, puzzling out the weave of the sackcloth
for nothing better to do.
Many words would go unsaid and sights unseen,
but money at least would not be a pressing concern.

London

We're here to beg from Uncle James, Mamma says, but he's not giving. This English city stinks. It grows and ferments. I love it; the city is alive and every house has books.

I've made a friend with a strange name. Sebastian Francisco de Miranda has taken me into his library and his confidence. He speaks to me of a new Venezuela, a country where men and women study together, like this is some commonplace thing. *I did not know of an old Venezuela, sir,* I say softly, and he laughs and shakes his finger at me in a gesture I don't understand. He is a friend of my uncle the painter. The one, Mamma says, who will not help us even were we knocking at Death's door. *And we are knocking,* Mamma says. She has grown reedy of late, and speaks of Death as if he were someone who will pay our rent out of kindness.

I am given to understand that Miranda is a revolutionary and a Freemason. I find a volume of his diary in a writing desk and read of escaping the French guillotine, of bedding Catherine the Great. We eat meat at his table, two Irish paupers sipping soup as quietly as we can. He talks of politics and his home. He hits the table with the flat of his hand and yells at his friends when they join us. Sometimes when they disagree they fight, throwing down their napkins and shoving each other against the furnishings. Mamma sits frozen in place until the storm passes. I watch the men, wondering at the countries that rouse this passion. Will I ever feel like that, I wonder. And about what.

After dining Miranda always has a book for me, and a place in his library to read undisturbed. My hands are small and white against the book leather. The library smells of leather and damp. The fire sputters day and night. I like that Miranda doesn't watch me read, doesn't want to sit with me and observe me in my study. Instead he just feeds me books, each following from the next. First it was philosophy, now it is anatomy—the latter much preferable to the former, for being observable. This latest is a book on the hand; I place my own hand on the page and trace my bones. Each illness has a name, a history and instructions for remedy. Each curve and corner of my body could be written out with a learned hand, and each name written has another name behind it:

clavicle	little key	
costa vera	true rib	
costa spuria	false rib	
costa fluctuans		floating rib
pelvis	basin	
os sacrum	sacred bone	
coccyx	cuckoo bird	
os innominatum		nameless bone

I feel for my floating ribs. At night Mamma cries and so I stay up late, unable to bear our bed shaking. There is nothing in our cupboards, we have no house, no provision or protection. Our relations are in debt or gaol. But doesn't she see it, the room I'm building in my head? One chair, a desk, a new book on my shelf each night. Dust in the air, a window letting in London light.

The idea

Who said it first? And how was it said?
Perhaps, your face at this angle . . .
These clothes, this way of walking, it could be done . . .
Was it arrived at by hints and insinuation?
The debts, the bad money, the gallery of unfortunate uncles with hands
    outstretched
through gaol bars, from prison hulks. Who at last took charge and said,
    there is a way around all this?
Father gone, house gone, brother gone, only myself and Mamma
    in London,
and we asked Uncle for money but he turned the question back upon us.
I was facing a long corridor, life as a tutor, a matron, a stale governess,
and at the end a merciful guillotine
as inevitable in its fall as sunset.
Who tested the wall of the corridor and dislodged the loose brick, found
    the unlatched window,
the hidden trapdoor? Daughter turned son, a mask at last
removed as I looked clear through the glass of the high window
and out over the street paced over and back by gentlemen.
Mamma fell ill; an ill wind blasted; a will drawn up; the trapdoor
    swung down:
a rope ladder descending into darkness;
a hole in the floor of the world—

New clothes

Mamma won't look at
me in my new clothes.
Tubes of cloth around my
legs, tight, and a tight coat
across my chest. I glance
at the mirror. The shoulders
are all wrong; the shape won't
cohere, won't flatten. I want
to cry. This isn't going to work.
A book of anatomy lies open
on the table. The curtains are
damp; I can smell them. The
room is cold. Mamma faces
the wall and hums. I run my
fingers over the back of the
chaise; it is split, the stuffing
is spilling out. I take it in my hands and pull.
Ribbons of fleece unravel.
I wind fleece over my arm, take up the clothes
and a needle and thread.
I sit on the floor and begin to sew.
I make myself a suit of fleecy armour; shoulders and sides.
The fire casts only shadows of warmth. Mamma paces;
she grinds her teeth then leaves with a creak of the door
and now in privacy I work on a codpiece,
cut strips from my shift and strap padding to padding,
unpick hooks and eyes and resew.
When I buckle it on I look like a cushion pushed inside-out.
But with the coat buttoned, the breeches tied—
well, the clothes are too small now—
but my shape is correct in the mirror, like a little toy soldier.
Buttons strain in their eyes. I wriggle out of the coat

and begin to let the seams out,
sitting cross-legged on the hollowed-out chaise.
I don't know where Mamma has gone.
There is a certain liberty in not caring.
My needle noses through cloth,
a wolf threading trees.

Journey to the university

The carriage is full of silence, on the road with Mamma.
She turns her mouth into corners; she isn't polite.[1]
We are travelling to the town where I am to study.
She doesn't want to be here, with me dressed like this. If she could,
she would lift out of her skin and slip under the door,
gliding through the grass until she reached the nearest waterway.[2]

I am going to university. She is not confident with her letters,
and secretly thinks most writing is only bad language,
perhaps imploration to the Devil.[3] She likes to assume the worst.
Her left hand is gnarled from where she once assumed the best
and my father assumed the worst across her knuckles with a stick.[4]
Her eyes are weak[5] and attract road dust. I am young,

I know what I'm about. I'm wearing my new breeches
and a yellow cravat. There are two ways of being,
looking in and looking out.[6] I look in, wondering
at the tethered, rocking boats,[7] the lighthouse beam
swinging across a new, ever-deepening sea.[8] She looks out
at the road, the passing hedges, the carved heads of cattle,
the men cutting sticks from a hazelwood tree.
Unseeing,[9] we sit across from each other
and eat a half each of a marmalade sandwich.[10]

[1] Politeness dictated I attend the funeral, but by then
[2] I was across the water, half a world away.
[3] I don't believe in hell and heaven;
[4] I think the form submits to slow decay;
[5] weakens with each year, its gait uneven,
[6] until to leave is simpler than to stay.
[7] Look across a mother's life, it is a continent
[8] with fractured nights and short cold-tempered days.
[9] An icy place, of mountaintops and dull depressions,
[10] sleeping villages and mourning day bouquets.

Code name

A life needs rinsing out, once in a while.
I live in a river town now, a Scotch town
and water runs through my house on April mornings.
It isn't really my house, but my real name
I wrote in the book by the door. The landlady watched my hand,
I think she thought me illiterate; small pleasure
in proving her incorrect. My code name is a real name
that anagrams to itself. Each letter denotes a number,
which denotes a house in my home town.
The landlady asks if I'll need meals, and I say I will.
The landlady asks if I'll give her trouble, and I say I will not.
My window looks across the street into another window,
where a woman teaches people to dance.
Some early evenings I see graceful backs
and necks turning in practice. I put my head down
and write the names of neck bones onto paper.
To sketch the bones of the hand requires the use of a hand,
and to remember the names
of the three membranes surrounding the brain
requires functioning *dura mater, arachnoid mater, pia mater*
(tough mother, spider mother, tender mother).
Three mothers, bones in my hands, a stack of books beside my bed.
The tenant across the hall from me does not leave his room
and a bad smell emanates from his door. I sniff,
trying to diagnose. I observe my landlady's gait and track
the progression of her rheumatism. I open the front door
(tough mother) and then the door to the stairs
(spider mother) and then the door to my room
(tender mother) and sleep, sleep. My name dreams
of writing itself over the tidy buildings of the town.
What will I do with this life, that I have in honesty
part stolen? Will I run through houses like an April flood?

Will I keep my membrane-cradled brain intact, the names of bones stacked like books within it?

The rules

Our world is not a house that can be walked
room to room. It is a web of rules, each strand almost invisible
and sticky, clinging, swaddling; blunder, fall,
err and one is trapped completely; panic descends;
one's thrashing draws attention and the great spider unravels
at the centre of the web, tracing terror to its source.
One sees her coming and her name is *Propriety*, her name is *Honour*,
her name is *Christendom*, her name is *Empire*.

The rules are different now. I travel unchaperoned;
I enter public houses; I attend a university.
Once I hid my hair and people would talk to me differently,
but now they listen differently too. Before they didn't listen
but now their ears are opened. I am worth teaching now.
I can be of use beyond myself. There is no question
of my right to board a ship, or take a room.
It is as though I were a ghost and I have now been given form.

The rules are different now. Honour takes on new meaning.
There is greater freedom, but one cannot run heedless;
there are still rules. For a year I barely speak, for fear
of speaking too loud or too softly, of saying the incorrect thing.
There is a way of standing, a way of laughing, a way
of touching one's friends on the back; but one must take care
to touch the correct friend, in the correct place, and not for too long.
After a year of study, I laugh. I reach out my hand. I count to three.

Speak like a man

Want to hear a joke?
A man wants to sell his donkey . . .
Want to hear a joke?
A sailor stuck head-first in a barrel . . .
Want to hear a joke?
A man wants to be rid of his wife . . .
Gentlemen, there are ladies present, pray mind your tongues
until we are alone and can speak with cruel abandon.
Want to hear a joke?
A Scotsman . . .
Want to hear a joke?
An Irishman . . .
Want to hear a joke?
A woman . . .
Gentlemen, now we are among men
we can break every rule we ever set for others.
Crinkle your eyes, set your jaw,
one hand outstretched *no!* to show you're really laughing.
Smoke has etched its tidelines on the walls of this room.
The carpet is pitted with burns
and the liquor cabinet locked to ward off servants.
Our host fetches the key hidden—clever fellow!—under a figurine
of shepherd mother and child
and I would bet money the servants know where that key is
and I wonder how they top up the bottles
but I drink anyway and set my jaw,
then lean forward, one hand outstretched.
Want to hear a joke?

Dissection

Every book on anatomy is written in blood.
My hands are soaked in blood.
My skin is sticky with it.

This body will not bleed, it is too old,
and the skin must be sawn open.
The black hair is crusted with salt.
Was this a person? Now it is a text,
the latest in a long line of volumes
one year or twenty years or forty years in the writing of it
and read over the course of a week
in a cold and darkened room,
skin, muscle, bone, cartilage,
organs growing more slippery by the day,
We are working against time, lads,
no rest, no rest. I am hungry for knowledge
and food, I surprise myself with how much I eat
but it is reassuring to feel the processes of digestion,
to remind myself that my body at least is alive,
at least for now.

What do the dead think?
Nothing, except perhaps their last thought,
a spider crawling through the slumping brain
the tunnel walls are close now but there is still a sound,
maybe an apology or a shout of love or one of those thoughts
that drowns out moments of narrative importance in real life:
When did I last enjoy fresh bread? Has the fire gone out?

What do the dead feel?
Nothing, thank the Lord, for the process of putrefaction

would be unbearable to endure in a feeling state.
Then there is the horror of the idea
that your body, which is yourself, is returning to the dirt.
Better that they don't feel, and that we don't feel for them.

What are the dead good for?
There is a religious answer, but we are men of science
and would say the dead are to be learned from.

Corner

I have a trick of making myself into a corner.
No one speaks to me then.
People pass by and see nothing.
I keep a room inside my head,
for late at night when I need a room like that.
I wouldn't want to do to anyone else
the things that have been done to me.
Is wanting the same as doing, if you want enough?
Why is doing like a static shock?
Who shook my hand, the night I forgot
my name and said instead some unsettling fragment?

ARACHNOID MATER

spider mother

Georgiana

She is taught French, but she cannot go to France. She is taught to sew, but only pretty things without use. She lives in a strange country and her mother is dead.

I am one day on the Cape of Good Hope, a doctor now. Her father Lord Charles Somerset asks me, is she ill? Will she die? What remedy would you prescribe? He has the wide-eyed look of a man confronted with a woman who won't get better when he tells her to. He is the king of this land in all but name. He tends the colony like his own garden, saying, plant here, weed here. But talking to me he is perfectly helpless. His hands twist in midair.

I attend to her. Of course, chaperoned. Her hands twist in her lap. She is a potted plant grown over-large, nowhere for her roots to go, and so she cramps, and wastes, and sighs. I ask how she spends her days and when she tells me I struggle not to weep. The tedium! the monotony! a coffin, cushioned and prematurely shut!

I ask her what she likes doing best. She says she likes music and to read, and when I ask what she reads she surprises me by saying that she likes to bring down her father's maps and study them, has done since she was a child (a nervous glance at her chaperone), and do you enjoy maps sir?

I say I do. I say map-drawing is a skill that can be taught, and perhaps your father could engage someone to give you lessons. She looks unsure at this, and the chaperone shifts in her chair, so I say in a stern voice that it is my medical opinion that she must find some occupation for her time, that her mind is over-active and must be exercised. *Much like the legs, ladies*, I say, and then I speak a phrase of Latin to quell any further opposition. *Map-drawing*, I say, *and*

long walks with your sister. I will speak to your father. And keep a
window open.

I tug at the latches and raise the sash. Sun-warmed air billows in and
Georgiana shrinks from it. I beckon her over and we lean into the
wind together, never mind the papers rustling behind us, the dust
whipped up and dancing around the room.

A month later I receive at my door a parcel. It is a map of my street,
each house blocked out. It is pretty work, too pretty, not practical,
but I have it framed regardless. With the map is a note from
Georgiana's father, inviting me to dine.

Two black horses

I lash my horse, cursing her slowness, while my mind turns over
cures. Blistering, cupping, copious venesection . . . Foxglove
to weaken the heart and bring down the blood. Steams of
marshmallow, camomile flowers and vinegar. I have little faith in
such remedies; prayer has shown better results. In my bag at my feet,
jars clink.

I am taken through room after room, bewildered still at the houses
of the rich. I keep my tongue in my mouth; no use panting like a
thirsty dog. Is this a second ballroom? Then hall, bedroom. The
hall is cool but the bedroom warm; someone has lit a fire on this
summer's day. People crowd the four-poster bed: old women in
shawls, three young men in a row, a girl creasing her dress as she
leans against the wall and fans her face.

I push past and throw open the bed-curtains. The invalid shudders
inside, a little white worm propped on pillows. She cannot breathe;
the room too hot and airless. I clench the curtains in my fist, then
drop them. Stare around at stupid faces, shoulder through to the
window, bully up the sash and let clean air inside. The pane cracks.

I say some things. Perhaps I shout them. The faces around the bed
don't change. I fling myself down, press my ear to the thin chest and
listen. I have to stopper my other ear to block out foolish sounds:
someone's mother won't stop crying; another hushes . . . I grit my
teeth and listen to the inner world of this woman, realising as I listen
to *thud, rasp, pump* that I've forgotten her name. I tap on her chest.
Her face is like a saint's as she watches me work. Tap, and I listen.
Tap, and I listen. I stand and demand silence; I stamp my foot until
they listen. Tap, and I listen. Tap, and I listen.

She lives. Her name is Mrs Cloete. She insists on paying me but I demur; I do not tell her that her case was not serious, that she was only pushed to extremity by over-heating, by heavy curtains and her family's ignorant concern. She sends me two black horses, tall and blinkered. I unblinker them and tell them there is nothing in this town to startle or fright. I ride each horse daily, in dry weather or wet. They are too big for me. I ride them yet.

Good words

Here are some rules.
You must be wary of good words.

You must know the date, but never the time.
You must be welcoming, but always with one eye on your sword.

You may go hither and yon, but you never escape your home.
When you eat you must be thankful,
and when you love you must be silent.
There are always more hours in which to be utterly intolerable.

A mouse in the wall. There are mice here, same as England,
same as Ireland.
They come on ships like men do. Ship mice become colony mice,
become Viceroy mice, become Cape mice.
There's always time for another change in perspective.

I should give some orienting details. It's night. It's always night;
when I have these thoughts I bring the night down upon myself.
Psyche snores at my feet. I have an urge to wander the town,
throw pebbles at windows, generally ruffle people.
My blankets scratch at me. I cannot sleep.

Yesterday I inspected a prison.
When I asked the prisoners questions their eyes slid left to right,
escaping my gaze, my interest. I wanted to know the truth
of their conditions, but they didn't see me as important.
They had their own hierarchies, their own ways of dealing with things.
I was a distraction from the tunnel they were digging in their minds.

With prisoners, with lepers, I have found the wall is stronger.
I mean the wall between myself and them. There is an elision,

a sliding over, a difficulty in grasping the other's meaning.
But sometimes I think the opposite: while the rest of us enjoy walls,
they have only bars, or wooden markers, dividing themselves
from the next themselves. I talk to them and my words hit
and sink below the surface. And their words come pelting back.

With officers I am unmanned; I am indignant; I am frightened.
I am appalled at what can be bought in this Empire:
position, title, honour, power,
men and women and children. I myself have no place,
and must skip from table to table, waiting to be offered a chair.
Sometimes I am permitted to sit for years,
other times I must flit, flit, keeping one eye on yesterday's host,
another looking to tomorrow's.

There are always more hours in which to be utterly intolerable.
Tomorrow I must file a report;
the conditions in the prison are insupportable.
People will be ruffled; they will ask who I am as if they don't know.
They will ask how soon I may be relieved of my post.
They will use words like ungrateful. They will use words like curious.

I always have one eye on my sword. It is a little sword, a decorative sword,
but I know the weaknesses in human armour, and when all else fails
there are always the eyes. I feel that if pushed to the extremity of violence
I would attack like a cat, all claws and teeth,
and like a cat be taken in hand and my brains dashed into the pavement.

A child is dying, drying, rung out like a rag.
Alongside her house runs an open sewer.
Did she play there? *Yes,* says the mother.
She was always playing in the river.

A slave dies, beaten by the Reverend's son. The autopsy says *Bulimia*.
I storm and rage until the word is changed.
Is that enough? A fellow slave had walked ten miles to report the murder.
Joris doesn't live, but the record is corrected
and his murderer is to hang. Is that enough?

I am wary of good words. Good words say that we regret his loss,
or that the child is with God. Good words do not allow for reformation,
for improvement. Good words prevent me from attesting

that washed hands or cleaned wounds, kindness,
or a proper system for disposal of excrement,
perhaps an ear bent close to listen to quiet speech,
would have avoided the problem entire.

Good words prevent me from sleeping, this night of all nights.

Into the ground

I have done many things
that would send my father
into the ground

if he wasn't already rotting.
I attend services at an English church.
I walk unchaperoned.

I have burrowed through the vilest gaols
and questioned men, native and Christian,
on their conditions,

the state of their food,
the state of their bowels.
I do not wear a hat

when I should. I have visited
with lepers. Sometimes
I wear a hat when I shouldn't.

I have acquired a peculiar reputation.
That I have required a reputation—that alone
would kill him. He didn't see me

and he didn't wish for others
to see me either. But now,
walking through the Heerengracht

I am seen with the Somersets,
I am seen at the theatre,
I am seen at the hospital,

my name is published,
my name is called, a name familiar
to my father, for I took it

from my painter uncle.
I gave this uncle new life in death,
something every artist wants.

In my doctor's way
I want the same, I want to live
after death, not in my patients

(who will often die before me)
but in my notes; which medical man
will turn the pages of my books,

following my process for caesarean,
treatment of malaria, treatment of cholera?
My dead hand will guide the scalpel,

my spirit will open the patient's window
and invite the breeze to disturb the curtains.
Father, I gave up even your name

and my chest burns with the righteousness
of that; Barry is the name I have chosen
to number my achievements under,

and your sad scion is a withered branch,
a forgotten, overgrown path
leading nowhere much.

Bonteboks

Lord Charles was sick, but now is well.
He sits in his library and dictates to his daughter Georgiana,
who once was sick
and now is well. The English threaten to impose duty on Cape wines.
He is angry. He speaks of vines, cellaring, fustage,
costs already sunk into the yellow earth.

A week ago he lay in a typhous miasma
and only I attended to him.
We were locked in; fed through the door.
In this cell I used my tools to their limits:
emetics, purgatives, glass of antimony, a watering can
to douse him in his fever nightly.
I took him to the edge of life and prayed
I would know enough to stop before I tipped him over it.
I was terrified, but I knew that if he died

and I had done not all I could
with this love in my heart
all the light in the world would shrink to a pinprick
I would break my hands under horses' hooves
I would open my skull and offer my brains to the sky—

Georgiana has lost her place; she is tired from much writing.
She asks me if her father should rest and I say yes,
to spare her eyes in truth. I escort him to bed, his arm on mine.
I have refused all nurses, the case, I say, being too difficult,
the treatment running along a knife's edge.
In his room, I shut the door and we embrace.
He sits, still weak, and pulls me weakly to his side.
He strokes my hair and asks what he can give me.
To be asked that, by this man!

The moment deepens. His hand is firm on my shoulder.
His lips part. I speak of the bonteboks,
there are so few now, their lyre-shaped horns so pretty,
and hunters cut them down ten at a time.
Perhaps a decree, I say.
My hand rests flat on his chest.
I only need to check. I use my physician's voice.
I only need to see where you are hiding.

Happiness

is a hospital running at full capacity, every nurse at his station, nails scrubbed, hands scrubbed. The doctor swoops in, alights on each patient, bestows a studied minute of attention, takes wing.

is the sea. Watch it race around the Cape, dash itself on the rocks. It is like being in the presence of a giant; a mountain moves and one realises it lives and breathes. But it is also a doorway; cross this sea and be in Bermuda, in Trinidad, in London, in Cork. And it is a city of millions.

is an excess of pus suppurating from a wound; the paleness of healing flesh; the patient's clear eye upcast.

is a bird bought at a market for nearly nothing, timid and furled in its wire cage, after ten days eating from one's hand, then hopping from hand to shoulder, black eyes taking in the room, and then an exploratory sally from shoulder to basin to shoulder . . .

is a dog at one's feet as one sits in the sun and with a knife pares an apple down to the quick.

is not a word I use very often. I don't often speak in languages of emotion. There is too much to do. But you asked me for a definition and I have obliged you, although all I could conjure were images of disconnected things: the familiar caged bird freed, the signs of productive medical practice. If we took the bird and added the sea, or took the dog and added the pus, or perhaps the bird and the hospital . . .

Which of these images is more to your liking? Which pleases you? Perhaps some are not ordinary, or not correct in your mind, in the light of your own experience of the world.

Myself, I like the hospital; it is where I am most days and it is there I feel a sense of purpose, an acuity of mind that brings the very paint chips on the windowsills into stark, colour-drenched focus.

But I also like the dog, the sun and knife and apple and quick.

Duel

The night before, my teeth will not cease
to chatter. My very eyes
shake in their houses. People pass by

unburdened, their honour assured, tucked
into their hats.
Should I aim for face or leg, or perhaps chest?

How to aim at all, with this trembling hand?
In the event
I hit him in the head, the bullet deflected

by his cap. He might have died. He hits me
in the thigh
missing (thank God) the artery pulsing there.

I dress the wound myself, fearing discovery.
Now my hands
are steady. A euphoria engulfs me, dizzying,

wild in its leaps from thought to thought.
I have honour,
and have given honour! I am alive!

Well

I am not a writer. I am a soldier. I am a surgeon.

Sometimes I write reports. I write in straight lines and use straight language. I would never dream of writing a poem.

Am I using words correct for my station? Am I using words correct for my place and time? Or have I slipped somehow, become displaced? It is so easy to count the years that one will never see. 1871, 1872. 1900. A surgeon looks at me from 1920, a year I pluck from the air and turn side to side. His mouth and nose are covered. I hope he sees something in me to respect.

Am I a liar? No. I know what I'm about.

I'm not accustomed to saying that.

I am a well. Or there is a well in my mind, clean stones, broad wooden bucket, rope. The water at the bottom of this well is so clear and cold it makes men drunk. It is black, because it takes the darkness with it when it is pulled from the well.

I would like to intoxicate. I would like to be a well-frequented well.

The rainbow ball

She dances with a Dutchman at the centre of the room.
Her skirts are pink and red. A rainbow ball, they name it that
for the people not the clothes; not just Dutch with English
but native with Christian, slaves with free men.
I look down at my yellow-lined coat,
my pea-green inexpressibles, my satin waistcoat,
a little stuffing round the edges to keep me in the right shape.

That slave girl, Sanna, says my companion.
*That's who caught your eye? Well. You know they say
she's a hermaphrodite.* I jump, the Greek word
like a midnight bell.

I don't listen to rumour, I say.
He shakes his head, laughing at me,
and I wish to be far away from him and his grey teeth.
I hail an imaginary companion and cross the room,
a gruesomely slow escape
for I must mind the dancers and observe
the peculiar hodgepodge etiquette of this place
requiring much bowing under outstretched arms
and pantomimed kisses.

It is months before I can purchase her freedom.
I must offer enough that Denysson does not ask questions.
He will think I love her, or want her in some compromising capacity.
Let him think that. To her I don't know what to say.
Leave me, I say. *Please, don't speak to me of this again.*
Please, I give you your freedom.
She leaves alone, leaving me alone.
I suspect both our faces are unreadable.

A shock to one extremity
causes the opposing limb to twitch.
I consider us connected, Sanna and I,
but I don't know what she thinks of me
or if she thinks of me.

I've heard there is talk of me in the town,
though I cannot hear it clear of confounding noise.
At night I walk down the Heerengracht and listen.

Some nights my legs are restless
and I think maybe Sanna is dancing
or maybe she is walking home to family
who may be very happy to see her, maybe not.

The surgeon's brain

It's not a trifling thing. A man's brain is, to some, the man himself.
Forget this soul nonsense. He has cut into a thousand bodies and
never seen a soul.

He has seen brains frozen, brains shucked from the skulls of
criminals, brains in jars. There must be brains in the bogs, he finds
himself thinking, Irish brains in Irish mud. There is something in
the bogs that preserves. Frightful bodies have been pulled from the
mire, twisted and browned like tree roots. Only the skin survives,
the innards drained and pulped by the bog, but he imagines the
brain laid in rushes, like an egg, like Jesus in the manger.

In an English church on an African Cape, his thinking stumbles
and he is a child again, watching from an upstairs window a beggar
walking door to door. She has a bad leg, that's what people say, like a
bad dog, just incorrigible. Young Barry wonders about that leg.

Later that night, he thinks about how his mind moved from church
to street, from Cape to Ireland. He considers a way to observe the
brain: a clean room and scalpel, a bone saw, an array of mirrors. He
would need assistance for the sawing but could do the rest himself.
He would not like another staring at his brain; it would be akin to
being naked. The limitation, of course, is that he could only observe
his brain thinking about his brain; he could not see what it looked
like thinking of roses, for instance, or of prison cells. Perhaps at
the point his attention shifted—he could catch that—the second
between thoughts. What would that look like?

It feels to him like there is more than just his brain inside his skull.
The brain is still but his mind feels as though it is always moving,
a shiny black spider picking through a web. This is why feelings
must be disregarded in the study of anatomy.

Living outside the brain of Dr Barry, as we all do, it is possible to make only a few observations. For example, we can assume his brain weighed between 1.3 and 1.4 kilograms.

He wonders whether anyone has ever been as unhappy as he. Sometimes he wonders if anyone has ever been as happy as he. Sometimes he dances around his room in delight. His dog dances with him. If you were to ask them why they were dancing they would no doubt say, *Because the other fellow was.*

He imagines a lecture. He holds a thin rod, with which he taps a blackboard. On the blackboard is the word HYGIENE. Under the word HYGIENE are twenty-seven numbered points. He takes his students through each point. The lecture is four hours long. When he finishes, the students don't want to leave. *Sir, is there more you could teach us? Please sir, we want to hear everything.* He chuckles, thinking about it, and decides to indulge them. His assistant rolls in a new blackboard. This blackboard is headed DISPOSAL OF EFFLUXIONS.

From where do these dreams come? Sometimes he is standing on a hillside, quite alone. An army mills beneath. His army—men he has trained from birth. He turns and runs and his army follows him, chases him, out of loyalty and bloodlust. *I taught you this!* he screams. He is lost to their spears.

Other times he is putting a child to bed. She is tired but strong, and hangs her arms around his neck. Patients call from behind the door. *They need me,* he says. *Please let go.*

I need you, she whispers. She opens her mouth and cholera climbs out.

He bounces baby Augusta on his knee. Her brain is growing fast.
When she was born, it would have been smaller than a clenched fist.
Since then it must have tripled in size. He doesn't tell her parents
this. They would ask how he knew.

Imagine a body without a brain. Monster. Demon. Ghost.
Imagine a brain without a body, not in a jar but alive somehow,
perhaps submerged in a pool of blood. How to feed it? How to
communicate? Would it be an it, or still the person it was? Is?

Dr Barry, he imagines saying to his brain. *Dr Barry, listen to me.
Today we have done something truly remarkable.*

The bad seed

A person, living at Newlands, makes it known, or takes this method of making it known, to the Public authorities of this Colony that on the 5th instant he detected Lord Charles buggering Dr Barry.

—*placard posted in the Heerengracht, 1 June 1824, author unknown*

There was a time when I was a bad seed,

but now I'm a bad tree
bearing bad fruit.

Rotting is something this community takes very seriously.
They leave me a note.
I'm not welcome here.
I quarrel, and leave myself around.
These are some of their complaints.

The demand is simple.
It is always the same. In every town,
the intervention.

Poison the ground, and the seed does not grow.
Blinker me and drag me into the river.
It's not easy, living here among you.
I'm frightened every day. But still
to live I must leave my quarters.
Appearances must be maintained,
or there will be more complaints.

Something this community takes very seriously
is education. I'm the kind of seed
from which children must be educated away.
There are concerns
about welfare. There is talk

of contagion. A bad seed only grows
in bad ground. Something happened
and now I am here,

a consequence of happening.

Lord Somerset departs the Cape

As you leave in your ship, and I stay on your land
I imagine a home for us in England, perhaps in Edinburgh;
a room that catches the cold morning sun.
We take tea and talk about the things we have seen,
terrible things, beautiful things, or maybe because it's morning
we only sit and no words pass between us because we know
we have the whole day set aside just for talking.
I take out my notes and lay them across the table, hospital improvements,
staffing, procedures, supplies, and you tap a finger on each page,
grunt in that way you do when you are surprised by a line of thought,
but you defer to me on matters medical
(yes, in my imaginings we live without conflict
my dear, none of these raised voices or shattered windows)
and the children welcome me as a loving

. . . Here, you see, is the problem, what do I look like in this imagining,
what am I to be called? And where is your wife,
is she bound behind a wall hanging?
Does she haunt the kitchens, the stairwells?
There aren't words for what I want, and my mind stumbles.
I give Lady Mary a garden, a green English garden
with white roses and high walls, so high she won't think about you again
or try to come to your door. In the night a thought creeps into my head
unbidden, a terrible thought, of shipwreck in the windy Cape seas,
and you washed onto shore, sea-clogged, dying. I revive you.
There is no one else around and you shrug off your coat

heavy with medals and water and say that you are no longer Lord,
and I am no longer Doctor, we may meet again as men.
But in this happy moment my mind is still busy
building rafts for the children to cling to, a rope must be woven
for Lady Mary to clutch, and there were others on that ship,
a whole flotilla must be summoned to drag them from the deep
and then there are procedures for chasing away the cold,
the rescuers will not know the correct methods,
even if they are medical men they will be lamentably ignorant,
at least the children I must attend to myself
as they will be cold and frightened
and they must be warmed and calmed
but not too quickly; that is the common mistake
and you understand I cannot entrust strangers with the life of Poulett,
with the lives of Augusta Anne and Mary Sophia.

Knife

A silver fish in my hand
sliding down the dead man's spine.
The finger of someone kind.

Estranged

We are estranged. We are made strange to each other.
We are made other. We are made over.

Stillness holds movement in it like
a set fire yet unlit, like a mountain.

Are you holding movement in you?
Are you moving towards me, like a glacier down a slope?

If I made myself over, could you come over?
If I made myself other, would we love each other?

I walked past a stranger yesterday.
I think he was you.

Winter holds spring in it, which holds summer,
which holds autumn. That's another year.

I travel to another hemisphere, fight,
quarrel, duel, bargain. That's another year.

What are you filling your years with?
I have only imagination.

PIA MATER

tender mother

Blood

Why do I tell you these things, Mother?
You are not even here.
You are far away and fallen in the road.
You reach out your hand to me
but I don't see it. You let out words
like air under water:

Daughter, come back to me, sit a while
in the road and let me comb
your hair. Your body grew in mine
like a vine, you found every crevice
and filled it with your bones.
Weeding you out was painful,
so much blood in the sawdust
they had to drag in another sackful.
They thought I wouldn't live the day
and now I see you striding ahead of me
with my soil in your roots still,
with my blood in your hair still,
I'm lying still,
you're lying still.

Why do I talk to you, Mother?
You do not hear me.
The grave is a locked door.
The dirt is a finger on lips.
Your ears are fallen into bone earrings
either side of your bone skull.
When I woke this morning there was blood in my bed;
not a child gone, only a month gone,
but I felt it like a child.

Imaginary eulogy

I have entered into detail as you wish, but I am unable of doing
justice to my more than father—my almost only friend, and am here
to be quiet today. Tomorrow I go remain till the earth covers a true
Christian. J.B.

—*Letter from James Barry to Emily Somerset on the death of
Lord Charles Somerset*

I have spent over a year in England,
cold and damp, Psyche shivering
at my ankle. I have tended to Charles,
kept him warm, told him not to ride
when he would ride, told him to stay indoors
when he would be restless. I am absent without leave
fourteen months. Ordered to Jamaica, but I would not go.

In his last week I accompanied him on horseback,
Tuesday, Wednesday and Thursday.
He was too weak, and he would not listen.
We did not talk as we used to.
Love is not something I can easily put aside
even when I see the faults in the man.
I am here to be quiet today.

John

I was awoken one morning by a sailor shouting.
A native of the region, he had seen in the sky-blue water
thick tresses of yellow weed, shining like plaited sun.
We had reached the Sargasso Sea. I would be warm again,
in the tropics again; as Charles' body grew ever colder
in English soil. No, I mustn't think on it (I told myself);
there is no time in this life for thinking of that body there
and this body here
for heating that body with this
for bending the world out of shape
to bring our foreheads to touch—

My new servant, John, wonders that I do not fall ill,
says he has never seen a white man so hardy to tropical disease.
When he says this, I wash my hands for luck
(still the superstitious Irishman)
and tell him I attend to the Blue Devil more than typhus,
more than sleeping sickness or yellow jack.
The rum is too cheap, he says, and I nod, surprised
to hear it after hearing so often from officers
complaints in the other direction.

I notice John noticing me, as I eat a breakfast of breadfruit
(unsure whether he is studying my peculiar appearance
or my vegetarianism) and he notices me noticing him
as he reads the titles of medical books that line my quarters.
We take on a study of each other, circling each other,
as I entrust him with more and more, first my clothes to wash,
then my pillows of a particular description,
giving my usual explanation that they are required
due to peculiar circumstances in which severe accidents have placed me.
I leave books open in my quarters, pages that might instruct,

or illuminate. We interest each other. We begin to trust each other. In a day we say perhaps five words to each other.
We don't know what's about to happen.

Rebellion

Outside the missionaries' chapels are burning.
In here, smoke filters through the shutters

left open to welcome a breeze that never comes.
Sweat sits heavy on the brow of every patient,

these men who waited on this island for years
for a battle where they raised guns against men

armed with knives and rocks, men who lit fires.
I have waited years for battle, an army surgeon

who delivers infants and vaccinates healthy men,
who oversees treatment of the drunken and venereal.

Is this what I have waited for? A few knife wounds,
a burn across an old soldier's arm, a bump on the head.

Outside the ringleaders, slaves and preachers and slave-preachers,
are hanged. In here, I try to make provision

for a room for yellow fever and another for dysentery,
but one cannot quarantine when one has only two orderlies,

and there is not enough fresh water to wash the bedding
or sluice the floor. A truly wounded man arrives,

shot in the leg, and five days later he is dead and dried,
dysentery wringing him from the inside out,

his leg healing nicely to no purpose.
This valley is a valley of death, the very ground

holds death in it, and I wonder I didn't see it before;
the sugar in our rations is laced with death,

and the bay is fringed with death,
and I scrub death each night from under my fingernails

sleep with death coiled in my hair.
Every second man in this hospital is dying

From early morning the sky is clear blue
and smoke hangs in the air. What is left to burn?

British soldiers set fire to churches
and the next day are brought to me trembling.

Doctor, what is wrong with me?
Doctor, may I please be sent home?

Their fingers are still black with soot,
rope-burned from pulling men to the scaffold.

The Cradle of Death

is what they call these thirteen islands.
My new post is Staff Surgeon of the Windward and Leeward Islands.
I watch over the cradle, rock it gently from time to time
when its inhabitant cries or fusses.

I begin to enjoy myself. I move to higher ground,
travel by steamer from St Vincent to St Lucia,
from Antigua to Montserrat,
install washing troughs in Barbados,
order the quarantining of convalescents,
remove lunatics from the prisons,
disbar quacks and outlaw the sale of patent medicines.

Late one night, John refreshes my guttering candles
and asks in a voice that is more like telling
whether I'll soon repair to bed.
The next morning I am unwell.
First fever and violent headache;
soon delirium and unconsciousness.
I have seen these symptoms a hundred times,

and seen their sufferers buried. I am carried to the hospital;
I will not release John's arm as I extract from him
the usual promises. *Do not wash the body,* I say,
and he continues calmly, for he has heard me say it before:
You will be buried in your sheets, if you are buried.
The hospital is clean, cleaner than I found it,
and the orderlies have been retrained by me personally.
They are nervous to attend to me now.
I feel myself sliding out of the world. . . I must trust
to John and to the orderlies, but they will not understand—
regardless. I must trust, though it is difficult to close my eyes

when such a tiger prowls around the room as this,
its great head level with my own skull half-sunk into the hay-stuffed
  pillow . . .

Fashionable bodies

I tease my hair ever more elaborately
and dye it red. It is thinner now,
and my hands are yellow, the skin sags.
Some dyes burn the skin,
colour the very organs of the body.
I've seen the staining of liver and lung,
the proud man's secret bared in surgery
but I paint and soak and rinse regardless.

They will not send me to the Crimea,
so I travel there on leave, a holiday
into the midst of battle. I tour the makeshift hospitals,
give my view on possible improvements.
I am a surgeon, I say. I am quite willing to be useful.
And sometimes I am ignored
and sometimes I am given a knife.

Soldiers dye their hair too, it's true,
and work for hours in the mirror
to shape hairlines, beards, the horror
of not being with the times only ever
acknowledged when the times are over.

We are dandies all, and after battle
the fashionable bodies lie in fashionable heaps
from that moment frozen,
and it may be only weeks
before fashion has moved on: living men
grow moustaches, change fabrics,
while dead men's bare lips cool and cling
to teeth of wood or porcelain.

I tend to an officer after battle. Blood smears his face
and his wounds are deep. He can't stop crying.
You aren't going to cut me, are you? he asks.
Doctor, it is not necessary to cut me. He is in terror
of the saw, but needs only stitches if I can staunch
the bleeding in time. His coat has ripped and I can see layers

of cloth tied around his stomach, a prodigious girth
squashed, his organs pressed, no doubt, against
the back of his ribs. *We must cut this*, I say,
touching the cloth. I take scissors and began to slice.
No! he wails. He clubs me with his hands,
too feeble to grab or punch. I nod to an orderly

to hold him down. The officer's eyes roll back;
blood pumps like it is under command to march out
at once. He dies. I take needle and thread
and sew his coat back up.

Eggs without mutton

I am driven half mad by loneliness; I see lit windows, a father moving
from room to room with a child on his back and I froth at the
mouth, I whip my horses and my wheels carve a scar into the road.

Foolishness! stupidity! to think I would not be left alone after all.
John comes and goes and completes my strange assignments, and
never asks what's in the box, or why must this person be paid.
Meantimes Psyche frisks about my feet, wanting to be soothed. This
Psyche is not the first, she is the third, each white, each christened
the same, each panting with a bottomless need for affection. *Here,
Psyche,* I say. I rest a hand on her head. *Here, have this.*

On the crossing to Canada I was chaffed for my pets, although I
had only brought Psyche, and one small bird cage, and of course a
goat for milk. I've learned to smile when people say things that are
disrespectful, or untrue, or which imply an intimate knowledge of
my life; I have become quite the mellow old man, until of course a
spark falls from someone's lips and lands on the hem of my coat and
I collapse into flames.

The boy with whom I shared a cabin (money being, again, tight, as
tight as in childhood) I would shoo out each morning so I could
change. One morning he was slow, sleepy, it had been a rough
night and he was rubbing his eyes and banging into walls. I became
enraged and struck him across the face. He loomed above me; my
hand had bounced off him like a stick thrown at a castle wall, and I
had a peculiar fear that he was going to break the porthole window
and force me through it like a cook forcing meat through a grinder.

My hand stung; Psyche barked at my feet. The boy apologised for
keeping me waiting, yawned and shuffled out. I walked bewildered
from door to bedside, then sat and took great gulping breaths.

Why do people not simply do as they're told? I fed my birds through their bars: glossy black seeds. My hands shook. I took so long to dress that the boy must have thought of knocking, but perhaps he didn't dare. Or perhaps he felt sorry for me. When I opened the door he was waiting, slouched against the gently rolling wall of the ship's corridor.

That same morning one of the cooks brought me a hot breakfast: eggs with buttered toast and greens, soggy but edible. *They were mixing mutton in with the eggs,* he told me. *And I said, mind you put some eggs aside for Dr Barry, for I remembered sir, that you don't eat meat. Mutton and eggs! Who's heard of that?*

The cook was young, with yellow hair. He reminded me of the Dutchmen on the Cape: big, broad hands. He clearly wanted to impress; he set the plate down and rotated it several times until its most pleasing side was presented to me. What did he see in this beaky old man worth impressing? I thanked him, and when I was done I addressed the head cook and commended the boy to him.

Which boy? the head cook asked.

The Dutch one, yellow-haired, I said.

You're the doctor, sir, aren't you? asked the head cook. *With the little dog and goat. And the cage of birds in your room.*

I confirmed the charges.

Which boy? he asked again.

I realised he was deaf, and I commenced shouting. He cupped one ear and tilted it in my direction. *He brought me eggs without mutton!* I shouted into the proffered ear.

72

Oh, I'm sorry sir. I'll have a word with him, said the head cook.

No, it was well he did! I screamed. *Eggs without mutton is what I wanted!*

He seemed taken aback by this. *Eggs without mutton,* he muttered. *Eggs without mutton.* He nodded distractedly at me. I gave it up and slunk back to my room. Psyche wished to walk about on deck, but rain had set in, beating against the porthole glass. *Stay here warm with me,* I told him (this being Psyche the Second). *You would not want to get your paws wet in that misery.* Psyche the Second was a sensitive dog and disliked damp, but had no brain for avoiding it. I had to take on that matter myself.

Stand your ground!

I am almost played out.
I'm in a new country, vast,
almost limitless and cold.
Children are born and old men die
and the snow continues down.

This child is not played out.
She jumps and runs, and won't listen to instruction.
She likes my hair. She says I'm red like her toy soldier.

I suggest wardship. The parents are a picture of discomfort.
I make my case: I have some money, a position.
I have a passion for the education of women.
She would have opportunities. I know I have lost them, already,
but I can't help it; the truth is I am lonely,
I see my position slipping from my grasp,
and every day the tremble in my hands deepens.

I am older than they think I am.
Old enough to be a grandfather.
The child thinks I am her grandfather.
As usual, in a household that is not my own,
I occupy a peculiar position.
I sit with the family for dinner. The servants are Irish girls.
Their pale hands ladle out portions.

The child wishes to meet my goat, so I invite her to call on me.
I feed her all her favourite foods: liquorice and penny candy,
she eats like a bee, all sugar,
and I let her look through my anatomical drawings
and show her the path of blood around the body.
She has an inquiring mind; it batters at her window.

I pull another book towards us, but she yawns
and asks for the goat. I open the door and call to him
and he comes running, his yellow eyes swivelling
to take in the room before alighting
on the strange child standing beside my desk,
and he lowers his head and charges
and without thinking I shout *Stand your ground!*
The child flies through the air
lands on a stack of books and shouts
Again! Again!
I pick her up and check for breaks but she's unhurt,
wants to fight the goat,
sure this time she'll win—
I wrestle the goat into the hall, slam the door,
sit down with the child and say
You must never, never, never, never
tell your mother or father
anything that happened here in this house today.

Every quarrel

I may as well warn you that you are to have a visit from the renowned Dr Barry . . . He will expect you to listen to every quarrel he has had since coming into the service. You probably know that they are not a few.

—*Dr Cummings, in a letter to Sir John Hall, Inspector General of Hospitals, 1855*

With the Landdrost of Rondebosch, who objected to my inspecting the prison in that region.

With Brother Leitner, the Morovian missionary who refused to improve the diet, cleanliness and treatment of the lepers at Hemel en Aarde.

With Carl Liesching, who applied for certification to practise as an apothecary without European training.

With Chief Justice Sir John Truter, who sided with him.

With Abraham Josias Cloete, Aide-De-Camp to Lord Charles Somerset, with whom I duelled with pistols; a dear friend.

With Deputy Fiscal Ryneveld, who objected to my request to transfer a man from gaol, lying in his cell with a broken leg and the other conscientiously manacled.

With Bishop Burnett, who asked me to relieve him of toothache as if I were a common tooth-drawer (I sent him the farrier).

With William Edwards, who I know placed that placard in the Heerengracht.

With the Fiscal David Denyssen who wished for that crime of damaging his property that a drunkard be declared insane; and who, when I refused, had me slandered, imprisoned and demoted.

With Sir Richard Plaskett, who assisted.

With William Gebhardt, who beat his father's slave.

With Dr Tardieu, who protected the same.

With Assistant Commissary General F.E. Knowles, who would not give me even money for sugar for the soldiers stationed at St Helena.

With Major Barnes, who attempted my arrest in St Helena over the sugar question.

With Major-General George Middlemore, who occasioned my second arrest at St Helena, on personal grounds.

With Lord Glenelg, with whom I battled three years over salary for myself and two able assistant surgeons.

With those two assistant surgeons, who turned on me while I laboured in the Windward and Leeward Islands.

With Colonel Denny, who threw my favourite horse-hair whip into the moat at Corfu and wished for me to follow it, in retort to my complaint that he drilled his men overmuch in the midday sun.

With Nurse Nightingale, so-called Lady with the Lamp, who would not listen to my views on the arrangements at Scutari Hospital, but merely squinted at me, wearing only a cap in full sun.

With Major General MacIntosh, who wished to cram ninety-three of my convalescing soldiers onto troop ships bound for Turkey.

With Lord Charles Somerset, who thrust me out the window in Newlands and dangled me over the hydrangeas when we were debating some matter I now forget.

What's in the box?

John holds the box gravely in both hands
while I wave my arms and stutter about what must be done.
Does Psyche bark? I hear something at the limits of my ears,
but John's face doesn't flicker and I know
that this sound is another symptom,
something else I should write down.

John is so close to me that when I stumble now,
I put my hand out for his arm and am alarmed
when I don't find it. The box is locked but he could pry it open,
or simply take the key, which I have made no great effort to conceal.
Or he could ask me, for the words, too, I have not hidden well,
they lie like worms under leaf litter that needs only sweeping aside
to expose them to the sun. But he will not pry, or take, or ask.

Everywhere we have gone together, from Jamaica to St Helena,
to England, Antigua, Barbados, Trinidad, Malta, Corfu, Canada,
he has made inquiries as to the food, for I eat mostly fruits now,
and as to the bathing facilities, for he knows I do not like to share,
and each morning he sets out a razor and cloth and basin
and does not comment that the razor never needs sharpening
or that sometimes in my haste I leave the cloth unwetted.

What life does one lead, in the eyes of another?
Does he see me as ridiculous, curious, barbarous?
Once in Antigua he was unwell and I wished to look inside his mouth;
deposits on the tongue, I explained, whether chalky or yellow,
were useful in diagnosis. He wouldn't unlock his jaw;
with a soldier's severity he kept his mouth shut and eyes forward
as I lectured him on the need for prompt diagnosis,
obedience to medical professionals, et cetera et cetera.
With another I might have been moved to shout or insult,

but with John I found my eyes welling, I was without defences
and I sat up half the night reading on symptoms and diseases.
I could hear through the wall his twists and turns.
In the morning he was well; his hands were strong
as he carried in the basin
and laid it on my shaving table. We didn't speak of the night before,
and I do not remember him falling unwell again.
Perhaps he simply never told me of further ailments,
not wanting to risk another lecture.
This is not something that has occurred to me before.

London

Out there, on the Cape, on the seas,
I was myself and the world was a place
needing setting to order.
Here the city has made me part of it,
its chimney stacks weigh on my head,
my body is a river bricked over and sewered,
soot comes out my nose and eyes,
food turns to grit in my mouth.
On the windowsill sit humps of soot,
and soot has turned the sparrows black
as cooking fires in every house are stoked,
and old women shiver and babies are born,
and children fall sick and doctors are sent for
to prescribe harmful and outdated treatments.
Epidemic diarrhoea; they will not say cholera,
but how many have died this week alone?
Hundreds in this city, and hundreds more outside;
water contaminated with the efflux of infected patients
this city
calomel and opium treatment
not effective
purgatives—castor oil, Epsom salts
not effective
inoculation with an extract of the plant *Quassia amara*, bitterwood
not effective
purging, beef tea or salt water
not effective
John brings me tea and I wish to throw the cup across the room
not effective
shit to death
sewers are important and should be the province of medical men
I will write a letter

I will write someone a letter
I will tell anyone who will listen
I see no need to adhere
to common convention when public health is at stake

Goodbye

Goodbye cup at my bedside, city fog.
Mist on the town, rain on the roof. Goodbye sweat
and tears and patients' impatient blood.

Goodbye waves. A hot day, and your family walks the shore.
Pebbles slide in your shoes. Love lives in my heart.
You've forgotten me, but I'm still here.

Goodbye clogged sewer.
When I look back I only see endings.
Was I a good doctor? A good man?

Goodbye bucking sea.
I'd rather die than hear the answer.
I'll die before I hear the answer.

Goodbye dew. Morning brings out the worst,
the best in me. The night had been long
and it was early, around four.

I'd thought there might be something more.

Elegy for medical practice

I will no longer listen to strangers' hearts.
I have given up life, and I will not save lives
anymore. I am now what is on the other side of medicine.
I am the drowned lung, the silent heart,
the worst of all possible outcomes.
I am what the father says when he asks
how long will this be for, then?
I am what the grown son says when he asks
whether there is something more that can be done.

Once I was a safe pair of hands,
a listening ear, steady eyes, neutral mouth,
a degree, a decree, a designation.
Now my knowledge is rotting out through my ears,
now worms are eating it.
I remember at the university,
cramming words into my brain until I felt I couldn't make decisions,
couldn't think of roast or shepherd's pie,
couldn't lie down because the words would spill out into my dreams.
I was building a library in my head,
strong men were working at it, sawing and hammering,
making a place for every book. And some of the books were medical,
and some were novels, and others I had to write myself.

It was only after the examinations
that I could sit down and idly leaf through pages,
really enjoy my library, sometimes enjoying the hot and sweaty men
who rested in the shade with glasses of lemon water,
sometimes just taking in the light,
so different from the cold of the university,
the endless rushing, the endless secrets,
in my library I was just me and I remember

arriving at the Cape,
how warm the air was and the light,
the light was just the same.

Rorschach

An incident is just now being discussed in military circles
so extraordinary that were not its truth capable
of being vouched for by official authority
the narration would be deemed absolutely incredible.

                We will never know all we want to about James Barry
                for the simple reason that he did not wish us to know.

*

Official report sent to Horse Guards that Doctor James Barry,
late Senior Inspector-General, was a woman.
It is said that neither landlady nor black servant
who had waited upon her for years had any suspicion of her sex.
Her motive said to be love for an army surgeon.
        As Barry's biographer, I was overwhelmed by the frequency
              with which the same question was asked of me:
                    Was Barry, in fact, a man or a woman?
            I felt like a midwife confronted by expectant parents.
The desire behind this question was to make Barry's life knowable.
           It seemed that there was no place for uncertainty,
               and that uncertainty was not a truth.

*

A medical career for a female in the United Kingdom
in the early decades of the nineteenth century
was unthinkable. The decision to live as a man
was apparently motivated
                    The evidence of the longevity
more by ambition than by identity.
    of this person living in the male gender in every way is definitive.

*

                              In our modern age intersexual people
                                claim the right of self-determination.
Perhaps her quarrelsomeness and hectoring manner
                              Nearly two hundred years ago,
was due to an inferiority complex
                              James Barry seized this right as his own.
which made her adopt an aggressive and uncompromising attitude.

                *

                              The secret of Barry's success
                                in presenting himself to the world as a man
                              lay in the knowledge of his experience that gender
She showed all her life that she was prepared
at the slightest excuse to quarrel with men.
                                      was a matter of entitlement:
                              Barry acted this entitlement with every gesture,
Was this revenge for a slighted love in her young days,
and was she an example of the inveterate man-hater
somewhat rare in history?
                                      alone or in company.

                *

█████ never could succeed in imitating the male persona entirely
—it was apparently not in her.
                              Erasing trans people from history
This consistent failure to shed her femininity
                              is an act of violence against our community.
is one of the strands of evidence against the idea

87

                  You deny our existence in the past

that ███████ / James had a transgender personality.

          and call our modern day existence a 'passing fad'.

*

Medical proof existed in the body
of the dead Inspector-General
that at some time in her life
she had given birth to a child.

*

                 Of the four possibilities of Barry's secret
      —that he was a woman, that he was intersexed,
            trans, or a homosexual, cisgendered male

Barry opposed policing of gender,
so I'd hope for same in her admirers;
               —the least queer possibility is the one
                 that seems to have carried the day

the evidence is open to interpretation.
        and won out in popular opinion.

*

                He had begged to be buried

The body is Rorschach.
      without any post-mortem examination of any sort.

Memorials

In 2013 a statue of Nelson Mandela was erected on the front lawn of the Union Building in Pretoria. The statue is nine metres high. It is the tallest statue of Nelson Mandela in the world. His hands are outstretched; he is smiling.

In the gardens of the Union Building stands a smaller statue, four metres high, which was moved from the front lawn to make way for the statue of Nelson Mandela. The smaller statue rests on a blank plinth. In the move from lawn to gardens the statue lost its name and also its spectacles, but it is otherwise in good condition.

The statue is of James Barry Munnik Hertzog. Hertzog died in 1942. He had resigned as prime minister of South Africa only three years before, on 5 September 1939, over his refusal to join Allied nations in declaring war on Nazi Germany. His government laid the foundations for the South African Apartheid state.

Hertzog was named after his father's cousin, James Barry Munnik, whose father was named the same, and his grandfather the same.

That grandfather, the first James Barry Munnik, was born on 25 July 1826. His birth was difficult; his mother Wilhelmina Munnik in labour for a day and a night. The midwife considered both mother and child would likely die, and so the doctor was called for. He gave his opinion that the child would not be born without surgical intervention—a caesarean.

Never in the British Empire had both parent and child survived such an operation. A Swiss doctor, Locher, describes one of three documented successful caesareans known to Western medicine at that time:

In order not to cut through the uterus exactly in a place where the placenta might accidentally be situated, and thus excite a violent bleeding, I chose a somewhat uneven part of its surface, and there made a little incision, so that I could introduce the index of the left-hand, to serve as a guide for the progression of the knife. The uterus was then cut open from six to eight inches along the finger. Immediately the child presented itself, together with its membranes, yet without any water. The haemorrhage till then was a mere nothing. The nearest part of the child was an arm. This, as there was room enough, was disengaged first from the uterus, and after it carefully one part of the child after the other in succession, and last of all the head. Already before the head was freed from the womb, the infant moved its limbs, and on the development of the head, to the greatest joy of the mother and all the attendants, it proved its life by loud cries.

All this done without the aid of anaesthetic.

The danger then was 'surgical fever' in the parent. Child and parent might survive the operating table, for the parent to die several days later of infection.

The doctor performed a caesarean on Wilhelmina Munnik. The child was removed alive. And Wilhelmina lived—whether through luck, or because the doctor who had attended to her always washed his hands, or because the doctor himself had first-hand experience of birthing a child.

The doctor, James Barry, consented to give his name to the healthy child and to act as godfather.

James Barry and young James Barry Munnik continued a correspondence for some years, until, according to Munnik family tradition, the younger James wrote to the older to say that people are talking about you around town, and that you look rather like a lady. The letters left off from that time, but the name endured.

Lying still

Am I a liar? Well, I have written things down,
and in doing so changed them into different things.

The biggest lie of all is an anatomical drawing,
organs laid out just so on a butcher's block.

Some would say my life is a lie, but I know
what I'm about, I know what I'm about.

I lied to my daughter many times, oh many times.
I told her the moon was a boat and I had sailed in it.

A poem with   missing

Something is missing. A story told is only half the tale.

Sometimes I keep secrets even from myself. I wanted
to have her baptised, but they said it was better
for her   not to be written down.
And so I don't write   down.

They say there were signs on my   , signs
I gave birth to a child. I look for her in Cork streets.
Each face a locked box, a life part-stolen.
In Canada I scour the Irish newspapers.
In Corfu I look for her.

Tell me, for what name should I search? I have a   name
known only to myself. I am losing meaning.
I am   meaning. The brain gives out,
in the end, the brain gives out.
This is the   ' of an imagined memory.
With all this love. In Antigua I   for her.

Why do I tell you these things? After all,   am dying. The brain
          ; the membranes cradle: mother,   mother,
          mother. On the Cape, that night, I cut the infant out,
the   pinned to the kitchen table. I am proud
of my achievements. No one else could do it. At last the   gives out.
With all the   in my heart. In   I   for

Notes and Acknowledgements

p.5: A statement made by Doctor Barry in his own defence against court martial for 'conduct unbecoming to an officer and a gentleman', 1836, and reproduced in Rachel Holmes, *Scanty Particulars: The Mysterious, Astonishing and Remarkable Life of Victorian Surgeon James Barry* (Penguin Books, 2003), 220.

p.51, 'The bad seed': The placard quotation is reproduced in Holmes, 130.

p.53, 'Lord Somerset departs the Cape': The anonymous quotation is reproduced in Michael du Preez and Jeremy Dronfield, *James Barry: A Woman Ahead of Her Time* (Oneworld, 2017), 211.

p.59, 'Blood': The opening lines of this poem are taken from the closing lines of 'This Room', by John Ashbery ('Why do I tell you these things? / You are not even here.'). From *Your Name Here* (Farrar, Straus and Giroux, 2000).

p.61, 'Imaginary eulogy': Quotation from Barry's letter to Emily Somerset reproduced in de Preez and Dronfield, 185–86.

p.75, 'Every quarrel': Quotation from Cummings' letter to Sir John Hall reproduced in de Preez and Dronfield, 341. Details of each quarrel can be found in that book, as well as in Holmes.

p.85, 'Rorschach': Sources of quotations are, in order:

'An incident . . .': *Manchester Guardian* (21 August 1865), reproduced in numerous sources including Holmes, 264.

'We will never know . . .': Holmes, 299.

'Official report sent to Horse Guards . . .': from the *Dictionary of National Biography*, reproduced in Colonel NJC Rutherford, DSO, 'Dr James Barry: Inspector-General of the Army Medical Department', *JR Army Medical Corps* (1 August 1939), 106.

'As Barry's biographer . . .': Holmes, 323.

'A medical career for a female in the United Kingdom . . .': C. Savona-Ventura, 'Dr James Barry: an enigmatic army medical doctor', *Maltese Medical Journal* 8:1 (1996): 46.

'The decision to live as a man . . .': du Preez and Dronfield, 422, fn 10.

'The evidence of the longevity . . .': Ben Power, curator of the Sexual Minorities Archive in Holyoke, MA, quoted in Samantha Risdel, 'James Barry Is Not Your Rorschach Test', *Them.Us* (27 February 2019).

'In our modern age intersexual people . . .': Holmes, 325.

'Perhaps her quarrelsomeness and hectoring manner . . .': Savona-Ventura, 47.

'The secret of Barry's success . . .': Holmes, 322.

'Was this revenge for a slighted love . . .': Colonel NJC Rutherford, 109.

'████ never could succeed in imitating the male persona entirely . . .': du Preez and Dronfield, 422, fn 10.

'Erasing trans people from history . . .': ZR/Zabé Ellor (@ ZREllor), Twitter (15 February 2019), twitter.com/ZREllor/status/1096067778287730689?s=20

'Medical proof existed in the body . . .': Colonel NJC Rutherford, 109.

'Of the four possibilities of Barry's secret . . .': Hamish Copley, 'Dr James Miranda Barry', The Drummer's Revenge: LGBT history and politics in Canada (blog, 2 December 2007), thedrummersrevenge.wordpress.com/2007/12/02/dr-james-miranda-barry/

'Barry opposed policing of gender . . .': E.J. Levy (@EJLevy), Twitter (15 February 2019), twitter.com/EJLevy/status/1096083868271013888?s=20

He had begged to be buried . . .': *Manchester Guardian* (21 August 1865), 3; reproduced in numerous sources including Savona-Ventura, 41.

'The body is Rorschach': E.J. Levy (@EJLevy), Twitter (15 February 2019), twitter.com/EJLevy/status/1096080977347076097?s=20

p.88, 'Memorials': 'History of a Case of Caesarean Operation', J.J. Locher, *Medico-Chirurgical Transactions* 9/1 (1818), 17–18; reproduced in du Preez and Dronfield, 215–16.

*

Many thanks first of all to Ashleigh, Fergus and the team at Te Herenga Waka University Press for turning a rough draft into a polished book. Thank you to Henrietta Harris and Russell Kleyn for the startling cover. Thank you Creative New Zealand and the Johnson family for funding me to finish this book and start others.

This book was sparked by the brilliant research and analysis of many, including Rachel Holmes, Grace Lavery, Hamish Copley, Alex Acks and Samantha Riedel, and buoyed along by my strong disagreement with other commentators, Michael du Preez and Jeremy Dronfield being at the forefront. Thanks to you all.

Thank you to Jadwiga Green, Etta Bollinger and Will Hansen for explaining how to write the truth. Thank you to Chris Tse and Jackson Nieuwland, whose books I used as guides over tricky topography.

Thank you to the family and to Anna for supporting me and for reading first drafts. Thank you Chuckie. Thanks Fizz. Thanks Prudence. Thanks Pippin. Thank you Eve and Bella. Thanks Cruise.